Guitar World Presents

The Bonehead's Guide to Guitars

**Published by Hal Leonard Corporation
in cooperation with Harris Publications, Inc.
and Guitar World Magazine
Guitar World is a registered trademark
of Harris Publications, Inc.**

HAL•LEONARD®
CORPORATION

7777 W. BLUEMOUND RD. P.O. BOX 13819 MILWAUKEE, WI 53213

Guitar World Presents

The Bonehead's
Guide to Guitars

by Dominic Hilton

ISBN #0-7935-9799-4

Copyright © 1999 by HAL LEONARD CORPORATION
International Copyright Secured   All Rights Reserved

No part of this publication may be reproduced in any form or by any means without the prior permission of the Publisher.

Visit Hal Leonard Online at
www.halleonard.com

- Executive Producer
  Brad Tolinski

- Producer
  Carol Flannery

- Book Packager, Designer
  Ed Uribe for Dancing Planet MediaWorks™

- Cover and Inside Illustrations
  Jim Ryan

Foreword

"Hey Paul, your birthday is coming soon! Have you thought about what you would like for a present?"

"Yeah, Mom, I want an ELECTRIC GUITAR!!!"

My first guitar was made from two pieces of stamped aluminum that had been snapped together, realistically painted, and shipped directly to my home from the manufacturer—Sears. The amplifier—included!—did not use a typical cable, but instead utilized a six-foot piece of yarn with a large SUCTION CUP that you were instructed to LICK before attaching it to the guitar's body. There was no danger of electrocution, though—the amp did not have an AC power cord, but instead ran on a GIANT BATTERY! I loved this guitar and spent many hours in front of the mirror pretending that both it and I could REALLY PLAY.

You have to start somewhere!

~*Paul Gilbert*

The author would like to thank Brad Tolinski and Paul Riario at Guitar World magazine, Jim Ryan for his superb cartoons, Ed Uribe at Dancing Planet Media-Works, Neville Marten and Sarah Clark at Guitarist magazine, Paul Gilbert, Bean and all those great geetar manufacturers for the photos.

About the Author:

Dominic Hilton is a freelance writer and incurable gearhead who enjoys spreading the word for Guitar World, Guitar World Acoustic, Guitarist, Bassist and Total Guitar magazines. He never has enough guitars.

Table of Contents

Introduction 1.

The electric guitar as we know it is a direct descendant of instruments that appeared 700 years ago. The guitar was, in fact, a bit of a slow starter and spent centuries competing for widespread acceptance against other instruments like the piano. However, due to its friendly nature and portability, the guitar continued to gain popularity until it became the most widely played instrument in the world today. A considerable part of this success is owed to Spanish guitarists, and later jazz and blues players, who developed the guitar as an improvisational lead instrument. Although this established it as an expressive and versatile instrument, a new type of guitar appeared that would redefine the sound of modern music.

During the pre-World War II big band period of the 1930s, guitars were blessed with electricity. Instead of ruefully playing rhythm to Benny Goodman's center-stage wailing, guitarists now had the power to step into the spotlight, and in the years to follow they did. The electric lead guitar and the rock guitarist ego were born, and all hell broke loose. During its meteoric rise, the infamous electric guitar has seen more variations and R&D than any instrument ever conceived. It has also produced many of the most influential musicians in Western music.

The aim of this book is to take you through the structure of the electric guitar and explain how it is put together and how it actually works. We will also look at how the many guitars available differ from one another in both sound and performance. This should help you understand and maintain your instrument, and stop it from ending up with the other junk in the back of your closet. With this knowledge you will be able to get the most from your guitar and join the thousands of players who enjoy the world's favorite instrument. Welcome to the family.

Construction

Although the many guitars you see racked up in the music store all look very different, they all have the same basic structure. The main parts can be summed up as the **neck**, the **body** and the **hardware**. However much these may vary in design, they are the essential ingredients of your guitar. There is no such thing as the perfect guitar, and the many different styles available all have good and bad points; it is important to understand these differences to find the right instrument for you. Guitars are described in terms of feel and tone—in other words, what it feels like to play them and what they sound like. These are very individual qualities, and if you are shopping for a guitar you will benefit from trying a bunch of different models to find those that suit you best.

Let's look at the basic ingredients, starting with the neck. These are machined from one or more pieces of wood and have a rounded back and a slightly rounded face, referred to as the **fretboard** or **fingerboard**. The metal strips on the fretboard are the frets, which allow the correct note to be played when a string is pushed down, or fretted, behind them. At the end of the neck is the **headstock,** which is where the **machine heads,** or tuning pegs, are fitted. The strings travel up the neck to the **nut,** which spaces them correctly at the right height, then onto the machine heads, which mechanically stretch the strings until they are in tune. The guitar has six strings tuned to the notes E, A, D, G, B and E. These strings decrease in thickness from the low E (the first string on the left-hand side of the guitar as viewed upright) to the thinnest, high E. The thicker E, A and D strings have extra wire wrapped around them to make up their thickness. These are called **wound** strings. The top three strings, G, B and E, have no extra winding and are

called **plain** strings.

The strings are anchored to the body by the **bridge.** There are various different types of bridges that we will look at in the next chapter, but all basically attach the strings to the body. The body itself is usually made of wood and shaped to be comfortable and easy to use. However, the guitar is about rock 'n' roll, so there are plenty that are designed to look cool, weird or fun. Expect to find guitars shaped like Cadillac tail fins, a map of Texas, or an alien weapon, but bear in mind that they may not be the easiest guitars to learn on. Whatever the body shape, the wood used and its structure, such as having hollow chambers, will affect the tone of the guitar.

The neck may be attached to the body by using a metal plate and screws (**bolt-on neck**) or by gluing it into place (**set neck**), or it may continue right through the body in a single piece (**through neck**). Once again, these different designs, and the wood used for the neck, will affect the tone.

Bolt-on neck

Set neck

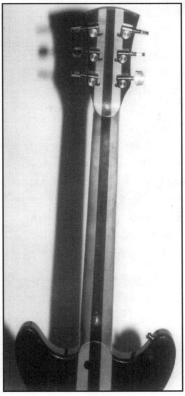

Bolt-on neck

The term "hardware" covers anything that is fitted to the body or neck. This includes the machine heads, bridge and **scratchplate** (the **pickguard**), which is a protective plastic plate on the face of the guitar. It also includes all of the electrical components.

Pickups and controls on a pickguard

Unlike acoustic guitars, the electric guitar uses electricity to produce all its wonderful noises. The essential component for this is the **pickups,** and there are many different types, each with their own sound.

Depending on the instrument, there will be one or more pickups, and these are controlled by various knobs and switches. All guitars have a **volume control**, which determines how loud the guitar is, and most have **tone controls** and a **pickup selector switch**, both of which alter the sound. The tone control changes the sound from soft and muted to bright and clear when fully turned up. The selector switch determines which pickups are on—those nearest the bridge have a bright and tighter sound, and those nearest the neck have a softer, more mellow tone. By selecting different pickups and altering the controls it is possible to get a whole range of different sounds out of one guitar.

Now that you've been formally introduced to the nuts and bolts of the electric guitar, let's take a look at four of the most popular design and manufacturing styles you're likely to come across and see how the parts and resulting functions vary from one model to another.

Fender Stratocaster

This is the most popular guitar model ever produced, and millions have been sold since it first appeared in 1953. This guitar has a bolt-on neck, three pickups and a **tremolo** bridge. Users and abusers include Jimi Hendrix, Eric Clapton, Dave Gilmour and Stevie Ray Vaughan.

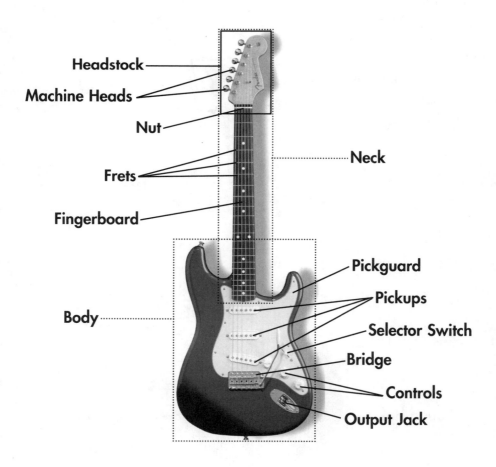

Headstock — Machine Heads — Nut — Frets — Fingerboard — Body — Neck — Pickguard — Pickups — Selector Switch — Bridge — Controls — Output Jack

Gibson ES-335

This is one of many models known as an **archtop semi**. This particular best-seller arrived in 1958. Typically these guitars have a curved top like a cello, a partially hollow body, F-shaped **sound holes** and a glued-in neck. Other sought-after semis are made by Epiphone, Gretsch and Guild. Semi users and abusers include Chuck Berry, B. B. King, Noel Gallagher, Ted Nugent and Pat Metheny.

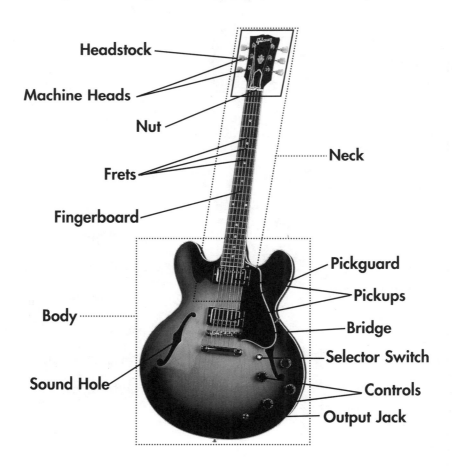

Headstock

Machine Heads

Nut

Frets

Fingerboard

Neck

Pickguard

Pickups

Body

Bridge

Selector Switch

Controls

Sound Hole

Output Jack

Gibson Les Paul

This is another model that has remained very popular since it was launched in 1952. The Les Paul has a glued-in neck and two pickups, and although it looks like an archtop guitar, it has a solid body. Users and abusers include Jimmy Page, Randy Rhoads, Gary Moore, Joe Perry and Slash.

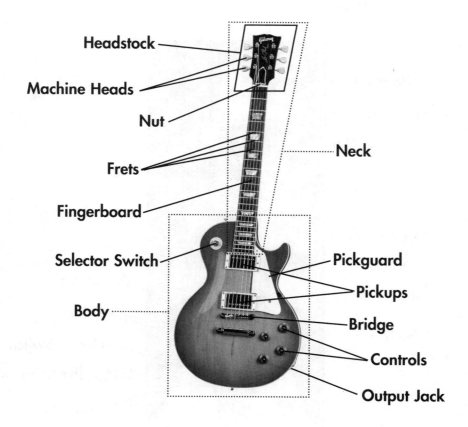

Headstock

Machine Heads

Nut

Frets

Fingerboard

Selector Switch

Body

Neck

Pickguard

Pickups

Bridge

Controls

Output Jack

Ibanez Jem

This a prime example of a breed of guitars that appeared in the '80s, nicknamed **Superstrats**. Companies such as Ibanez, Jackson, Hamer and Kramer designed guitars based on the Stratocaster but aimed at rock and metal players needing better tuning stability and aggressive pickups. Note the carry handle and unusual trim. Superstrat users and abusers include Steve Vai, Eddie Van Halen, Joe Satriani, Kirk Hammett and Paul Gilbert.

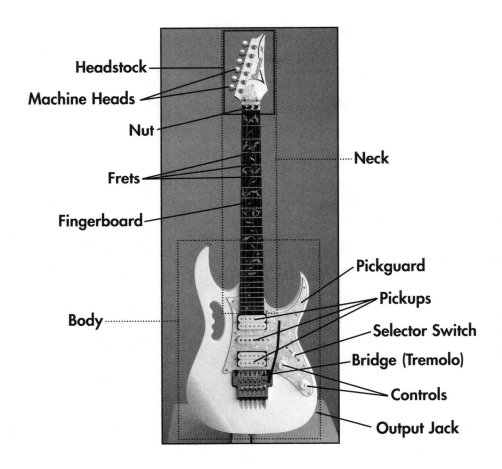

- Headstock
- Machine Heads
- Nut
- Neck
- Frets
- Fingerboard
- Pickguard
- Pickups
- Body
- Selector Switch
- Bridge (Tremolo)
- Controls
- Output Jack

How They Work **3**

In this chapter we will look at the components of the guitar in more detail and see how they actually work. By understanding how these parts function you'll get the most from your instrument and be able to maintain it properly.

Neck

The neck is a very important part of the guitar, as it defines a large part of the feel. The shape of the back of the neck is called the **profile**, and it ranges from a shallow 'C' shap, to fatter 'D' shapes and even quite pronounced 'V' styles. The width of the neck flares out from the nut to the last fret, and these dimensions can also vary. The human

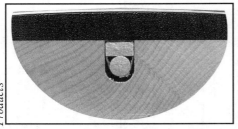

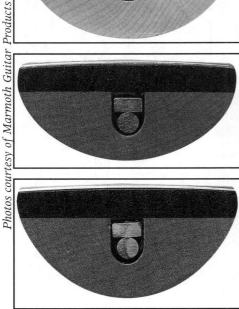

Photos courtesy of Marmoth Guitar Products

hand can detect minute changes in size, so it is important to try a number of necks to find one that feels comfortable to your hand, even though they may all look the same.

Another important dimension is the **radius** of the fretboard, or how curved it is. Older guitars have smaller radii such as $7\frac{1}{2}$" or 9", which produce a more curved fretboard. Modern guitars tend to be about 12", which gives a flatter fretboard. The more curved a fretboard, the more comfortable it is to play chords, but a flatter curve makes lead playing,

Different neck profiles

especially string bending, easier. Usually beginners find shallow, wide necks with a large, less curved radius easier to learn on. Some companies, such as Yamaha, produce guitars with **compound radii**, so the nut end of the neck is more curved than the top end, giving the player the best of both worlds.

Necks are usually made from dense hardwoods, such as **maple** or **mahogany**, although companies have experimented with other materials such as carbon fiber and aluminum. Woods used in neck construction are tough and stable but still need extra support due to the great tension exerted by the strings. This support comes from a **truss rod**, which is a metal rod fitted inside the neck along its length. The truss rod is slightly curved and pulls the neck away from the strings to keep it straight. The tension can be adjusted by a bolt that is either located by the nut on the headstock (often under a plastic cover) or at the end of the neck where it joins the body. If the neck bows slightly it can cause the strings to sound buzzy, and the truss rod needs to be adjusted. It is best to have a qualified repairman do this as it is a delicate procedure.

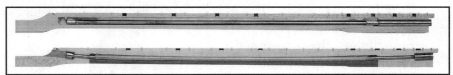

Cross-section showing truss rod (courtesy of Marmoth Guitar Products)

Fretboard and Frets

If the fretboard is a pale color then it is maple, which is common on bolt-on necks. A dark fretboard will usually be rosewood or ebony, which are extremely hard woods that resist wear from playing. A neck with a maple fingerboard will add a slightly brighter, more punchy tone to a guitar than one with ebony or rosewood. The dots, rectangles or

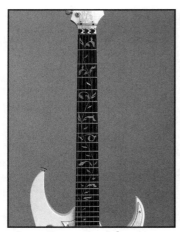

Decorative inlays

other shapes fitted into the fretboard are **fret markers**. These help you navigate around the neck as you play and are made from black or white plastic, fake mother-of-pearl ("pearloid") or real mother-of-pearl.

Frets are made from nickel silver or pure stainless steel. They are rounded on top with a vertical, toothed strip (**tang**) on the underside, which secures the fret into the **fret slot**. The shape of the fret can vary from the thin, high wire found on old Fender guitars to wide, flat wire found on many Gibsons. The **jumbo** fret is common on modern instruments and is both tall and wide, which is ideal for demanding, modern rock techniques. The frets will also play a part in the feel of a guitar and are yet another factor that affects the character of the instrument. The frets are spaced in such a way that they gradually get closer together as they reach the body. This is done to ensure that each of the frets are in tune relative to one another when played. These measurements are calculated from a mathematical equation written by the mathematician Pythagoras in 500 B.C. It is worth knowing that guitar necks are not all the same length, which determines the

scale, measured as the distance between the nut and the bridge. For example, Gibson guitars traditionally have a shorter scale than Fender guitars, giving the strings a 'bendier' feel.

Traditionally, Fender guitars have 21 frets and Gibsons have 22, although modern Fenders now also have 22. It has become increasingly common for guitars to have 24 frets, allowing a full two octaves to be fretted on each string. In theory a guitar can have as many frets as is possible to fit on the neck before they get too close together to play. Washburn had some success with guitars that featured an extended cutaway and a total of 36 frets, offering up to three octaves on the higher strings.

Nut

As previously explained, the main function of the nut is to

Plastic nut

space the strings correctly at the right height from the fretboard. However, not all nuts are created equal. The most common materials used for nuts are plastic, bone and occasionally brass or aluminum. Modern instruments may also use a material that contains **graphite**, which is naturally slippery and can help prevent strings from fouling and going out of tune.

Recent developments in this area have produced mechanical nuts that virtually eliminate troublesome friction.

Graphite nut

Wilkinson roller nut

Companies such as Wilkinson and LSR offer metal nuts with roller or ball-bearing mechanisms that allow the strings to move freely. This is especially useful for tremolo-equipped guitars. Another type of nut that appears on modern rock guitars has the ability to lock down the strings. If the guitar is equipped with a Floyd Rose tremolo or another similar design, there will be three clamps in place of the nut, which prevent the strings from moving at all once tuned. Although this works in the opposite way than a roller nut, the tuning stability is

LSR roller nut

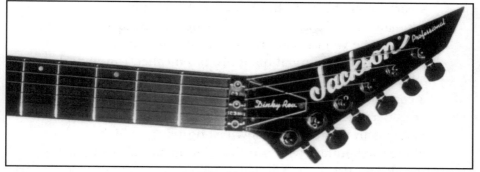

Locking nut

exceptionally good, and guitars have been known to remain in tune with this system even after the headstock was broken off—a truly amazing occurrence.

Body: Material

The main concern for the body of an electric guitar is simply to connect the neck to the bridge and the pickups, and, ultimately, the strings to the finger bones. As such, the shape and materials of bodies vary considerably, but most are made of wood and shaped for comfort.

Wood makes an ideal material for guitar bodies as it can be easily machined and is attractive. Also, the microscopic structure of the grain has bundles of tiny tubes that resonate in sympathy with the strings to produce a pleasing sound. The woods that are most commonly used are hardwoods with good tonal qualities, often called **tonewoods**. These woods all have different properties and are chosen for a combination of tone, appearance and manufacturing considerations. Some of these woods have eye-catching patterns in their grain, known as **figuring**, which are chosen for guitars with see-through finishes. This figuring usually occurs in woods that are slow-growing or from exotic regions. As such they can add a considerable cost to the finished guitar.

Table 1 compares the most common guitar woods in terms of their appearance, sound, cost and other characteristics.

Some guitars may be made from a single piece of wood, but more usually they are constructed from two or more pieces of the same wood, which are glued together before the body is shaped. Cheaper guitars may use as many as seven pieces to save on production costs, or even use a laminate—a type of high-quality plywood. Some guitars also incorporate several different woods in their construction for a combination of tone, strength and cosmetics. The most common example of this is a **figured maple cap**.

Maple caps are favored due to the attractive figuring that can occur in the grain. These patterns can be **flame**, **quilted** or **bird's-eye** and are particularly sought after. The cap is a 1-

to-2-cm slab of wood that is glued onto the front face of the body, and the maple's bright tone is used to produce a more balanced sound when combined in this way with softer-sounding woods such as mahogany. These figured caps are usually made from a single piece of wood that has been split down the middle, then opened like a book and fitted by matching the two sides down the center line of the body. This technique is called bookmatching, and can be seen on guitars like the Les Paul.

Wood Type	Appearance	Tone	Cost	Characteristics
Mahogany	reddish-brown, sometimes with attractive grain	thick and warm with good sustain	quite expensive due to its increasing scarcity	heavy and dense
Ash	cream-colored, often with dramatic grain patterns	bright with good sustain	relatively inexpensive	heavy and very hard, difficult to finish, which adds to the cost of the instrument
Alder	light brown with little figuring	balanced and full	one of the least expensive tonewoods	light in weight, easy to finish—a popular body wood
Maple	can be almost white in color	very bright with "bite" and long sustain	relatively inexpensive	heavy and dense, not usually used for bodies but very common for necks
Rosewood	very dark brown	similar to maple but warmer	can be very expensive	very heavy, normally used for fingerboards, occasionally for bodies
Korina	mid-brown with distinct grain	warm and full with good sustain	a fairly expensive, exotic wood	medium weight, suits transparent finishes
Koa	very attractive, rich black-brown grain	warm with a balanced brightness	expensive—it grows only in Hawaii	fairly heavy, always has a transparent finish
Basswood	pale and fairly unattractive	a rounded, warm tone	one of the cheapest and most common tonewoods	lightweight and soft but with good tone—perfect for solid finishes

Table 1

Due to pressure from environmental groups, many guitar manufacturers use timber from a sustainable source and some have introduced untraditional tonewoods, like sycamore, for this reason. There are also methods that produce the look of exotic woods without the financial or ecological cost by using thin figured **veneers** over standard wood, or by using a three-dimensional photographic technique to mimic expensive woods. If a body is finished in a solid color, then the tone of the wood is the major consideration; if the finish is transparent, then a tonewood with a more interesting grain is preferred. This may be common ash, or more exotic woods such as koa and African lacewood—the choice is naturally reflected in the price of the instrument. It doesn't always follow that expensive woods sound as good as they look. A cautionary tale from a renowned repairman who was knocked out by the incredible tone of a Strat that arrived in the workshop: When he dismantled the guitar he found that it had a replacement body made from nothing more exotic than cheap plywood. His advice? Shop with your ears as well as your eyes.

The whacky science of guitar building has led to manufacturers' trying all sorts of alternative materials for bodies. Various degrees of success were had with cast aluminum, metal tubing, transparent plastic and high density fiberboard (a solidified mix of glue and sawdust that works surprisingly well). A clear winner is Steinberger, which uses space-age resin and carbon fiber composites to make its minimal, head-less—and virtually body-less—guitars and basses. A less successful attempt was made by a now-defunct U.K. company that built guitars with solid marble bodies. Heavy rock, perhaps; backache, certainly.

Body: Shape

Unless the guitar has hollow chambers in the body or another similar semi-solid structure, a guitar with a solid body can be whatever shape the designer dreams up. Most bodies are shaped to be user-friendly in seated or standing positions, as well as pleasing to the eye.

All solid-body guitars have either single or double **cutaways** that allow the player's fretting hand to easily reach the upper frets of the fingerboard. In addition, the body is usually contoured to fit comfortably on the knee for playing while sitting down. This doesn't have to mean the guitar is conventionally shaped. Gibson's Explorer is an ergonomic design that is still pretty out there by today's standards. It first appeared in 1958 along with their Flying

V and Moderne guitars, but was considered too futuristic and was discontinued the following year. Then, due to demand, it was reintroduced in the 1970s.

Since those early days guitar manufacturers and custom builders have snubbed convention with designs from the unusual to the ridiculous. Normally reserved for live and video appearances, these weird beasts may not be ideal for jamming on the couch but certainly attract attention at gigs.

Affordable weirdness can be had from many companies nowadays. Some notable ones are by BC Rich, with their gothic spiked Bich and Mockingbird models. Jackson also has a

Gibson Explorer

Rick Nielsen's Hamer

production oddity in the shape of the alien-inspired Roswell Rhoads, which is made from machined aluminum with crop-circle inlays. The American Showster is shaped like a Cadillac tail fin, complete with a working brake light that is activated by the trem.

Other crowd-pleasers include ZZ Top's furry Deans, with built-in TVs, Steve Vai's ambidextrous triple-necked Ibanez in the shape of a heart, and Bo Diddley's cool rectangular Guild. Also quite notable is "The Beast" Hamer owned by Cheap Trick's Rick Nielsen, with its wild design and five necks. And of course we can't forget to mention all those crowd-pleasing favorites with the on-board speedometers, disco lights and rocket launchers.

Body: Finish

The finish on a guitar is inevitably a big factor in a purchase, even if only because it looks good. There is some argument that thin or **non-lacquered** finishes improve tone, but this remains to be proved. The most common finishes are solid colors, transparent lacquers and the more traditional **sunburst**, which subtly changes from clear in the center to solid color at the edges of the body. All of these finishes are sprayed onto the guitar and built up with a number of coats before being polished and buffed. Apart from giving the guitar a sleek, glossy sheen, they also do a good job of keeping the elements away from the wood to protect the instrument, although even the best are not swimming-pool-proof.

Another alternative is an **oiled** finish that uses tung or similar oil to seal and waterproof the wood. This produces a very natural look and feel to the wood and enhances the grain much like a clear lacquer. More unusual coverings include floral designs, found on some Fender and Ibanez guitars, which are applied in a sheet then sealed with lacquer. The ESP guitar company also experimented with the same technique to adorn bodies with dollar bills and Batman comic strips. As with body shapes, there are plenty of freaky finishes, too: snakeskin, sheet metal, airbrushed goblins, polka dots and rhinestones, to name but a few. It's simply a matter of taste, or lack of it.

Bridge: Fixed

Bridges fall into two distinct categories: **fixed** and **tremolo**. A fixed bridge can be a single unit or divided into a bridge with a separate **tailpiece**. For example, the single-unit bridge on a Fender Telecaster has the strings fitted through the back of the body, which then pass through holes in the face of the bridge. The Gibson Les Paul has the strings attached to a separate tailpiece before they travel over the bridge. Whichever style of fixed bridge is used, they are favored by players looking for improved sustain with a punchy sound. Tuning also tends to be more reliable on a fixed-bridge model, as the strings move very little in comparison with a tremolo unit.

All bridges have some type of **saddles**, which are pieces of metal shaped to carry the strings over the bridge. In most cases they can be adjusted for height and moved back and forth. The height adjustment determines the distance between the string and the tops of the frets, a measurement referred to as the **action**. Most players prefer a low action, which is easier to play; more experienced players may have a higher action, which improves tone and sustain. The back-and-forth adjustment is used to alter the **intonation** (see box out). These two sets of adjustments are vital to ensure the guitar plays well and in tune. The process of making these adjustments is the greater part of what is termed the *setup*—a service your guitar should be treated to periodically to keep it playing at its best.

Intonation

At this point we need to briefly delve into the slightly confusing world of intonation. As already mentioned, the distance between the nut and bridge is called the scale. This measurement determines where the bridge is fitted, with the midpoint between the bridge and nut being the **12th fret**. The laws of physics dictate that when a string is halved—i.e., played at the 12th fret on a guitar—it will vibrate at twice the speed, producing a note an octave higher. From this basic law Pythagoras was able to produce his formula that allowed guitar builders to calculate how the frets should be spaced so that they played equal musical steps, or **semitones**. Clever though his formula is, it doesn't work perfectly in the real world, and that is what intonation is all about. Due to the differences in string tension and pitch, the overall length of the string must be tweaked to get it to play in tune up and down the neck. This is done by moving the saddles backward or forward until the gremlins are gone and the tuning sounds sweet. That covers the mechanics of intonation, but if you want more information, check out any number of beginner's books for a more detailed explanation of the theory.

Bridge: Tremolo

Whatever you call it—tremolo, trem, whammy, wang-bar—this is one fun piece of machinery. One of the first effects available to the guitarist, this clever bit of hardware allows the tension of the strings to be altered, thereby changing their pitch. This enables you to add subtle modu-lations to chords and texture to passages, or to create wobbly sonic mayhem like Hendrix or Van Halen. Most tremolos work by having the bridge balanced on a **fulcrum** between the tension of the strings and some heavy springs in the rear of the guitar. By pushing or pulling on the tremolo arm you can change the pitch of the strings.

Modern Fender tremolo

When you let go, the springs pull the bridge back to its original position and tuning.

There are an increasing number of tremolo systems available, with new models appearing every year. These can

Tremolo springs in guitar's rear cavity

36

be split into two groups; the **vintage** styles and the **modern** styles. Vintage systems are reproductions of original units such as the **Bigsby** and **Fender "Synchronized" tremolos**. These offer an authentic feel and tone for players who prefer traditional styles and tend to work best for subtle use. When players like Hendrix inspired guitarists to go crazy with these older

Vintage Fender tremolo

systems, tuning stability became a problem as the strings would slip after such heavy-handed whammy stunts. Since then, companies have refined these original designs to help solve the tuning problems. One breakthrough was the **Floyd Rose** system, which locks the strings in place at both ends. The nut we have already covered; the bridge requires that the **ball-end** of the string is clipped off and the cut end clamped into the bridge. Effective as this

Floyd Rose locking tremolo

system is, it proved to be rather fiddly to retune, so **fine-tuners** were added to the bridge, allowing any wandering

Wilkinson tremolo

Bigsby tremolo

strings to be tuned without having to unclamp the nut. This improved design was very successful and was also licensed by Floyd Rose. It appears in various forms on such guitars as Ibanez, Hamer, Washburn and BC Rich. Since then, companies have tried to combine various clamping, low-friction and roller-type designs to optimize tuning stability, but without the bulk and complexity of the Floyd Rose. Best-selling versions include the streamlined Wilkinson tremolo and the hybrid **Blanda-Floyd** system.

It is important to realize that any tremolo system will also affect the tone of a guitar. Unlike a fixed bridge, the strings are not attached directly to the body and produce a looser, more "airy" tone. Some players prefer this subtle difference in sound even if they don't use the tremolo as part of their

Modern Blanda-Floyd tremolo

technique. A good example is Eric Clapton, who uses a Fender Stratocaster fitted with a modified tremolo. As Eric doesn't use the trem, he has the arm removed, extra springs put in the back, and the tremolo blocked from moving by a small piece of wood. This gives him the tone of a tremolo guitar with the stability of a fixed bridge.

Machine Heads

Vintage-style Fender machine heads

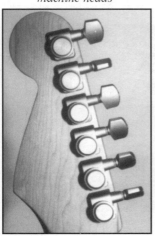

Sperzel locking machine heads

Also known as **tuning pegs** or **tuning keys**, the machine heads mechanically wind the string onto a post, enabling the guitar to be tuned. The earliest versions were nothing more than a wooden peg in a hole, but these days precision-made gears make tuning quick and reliable. **Sealed machine heads** are considered the best for electric guitars as their self-lubricating mechanism offers a smooth and accurate tuning. There are a number of companies that specialize in quality machine heads, such as Grover and Schaller, but most guitar manufac-turers opt to make, or commission, their own brand. One style of machine head that is becoming increasingly popular, especially on tremolo-equipped guitars,

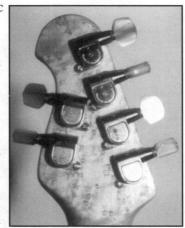

Modern Schaller machine heads

is the **locking** type. The most popular of these are the
Sperzel or Schaller versions, which both use a thumbwheel
to lock the string in place with a minimum of winding on
the post. This helps to eliminate tuning problems while
making string replacement very easy.

Pickups

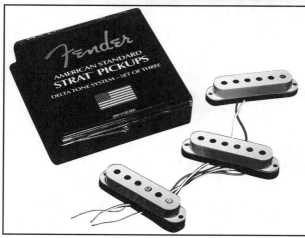

Single-coil pickups

The pickup can
be thought of as
the dynamo of
your guitar, as it
generates the
electricity that, in
turn, captures
and amplifies the
resonant charac-
teristics of the
instrument. You
may recall from
physics class that
when a wire
moves through a magnetic field it produces electricity. As
dull as that may sound, it is the essence of the pickup and
the sound of rock 'n' roll. The pickup uses a **magnet** and a

coil made from
thousands of
turns of wire no
thicker than a
human hair. This
produces a
magnetic field,
and when the
string vibrates
within it, elec-

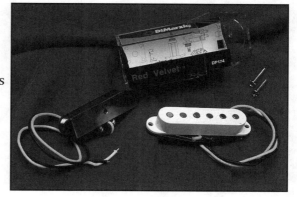

40

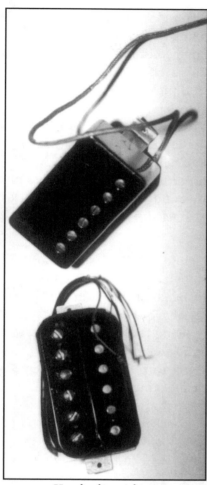

Humbucker pickups

tricity is produced in the coil, which then becomes sound when fed through an amplifier.

As simple as the pickup is, it has become a hotbed of debate, with hundreds of different variations appearing over the years. However, all pickups can be divided into one of two types: **single-coil** or **dual-coil humbucker**. The single-coil is so called because it uses a single coil of wire as the basis for its structure. These pickups are usually associated with Fender guitars, although the first pickup appeared on a Rickenbacker guitar in 1931, with Gibson debuting their version in 1934. Both of these designs were single-coil. The Fender Stratocaster pickup has become the most popular design for single-coil units, using six individual magnetic **pole pieces**—one under each string—and a coil with about 8,000 turns of wire. This design produces the trademark punchy bite associated with single-coil-equipped guitars.

The first humbucker was invented in 1955 by a Gibson designer called Seth Lover. His design used two single coils wired together with a common magnet underneath. The coils are wrapped around a **bobbin**, in the center of which are the pole pieces. One set of pole pieces was plain, the other was adjustable, with screw heads to fine-tune string-to-string output. The really clever thing about Lover's design was the way in which the coils were wired together. It allows the current to flow from one coil to the other **(series wiring)** but to move through each coil in opposite directions **(out of phase)**. Single-coil pickups are notoriously susceptible to background interference, especially mains hum, but due to its wiring, the humbucker eliminates this noise, literally "bucking the hum." This design allows guitarists to play at high volume and gain with a minimum of unwanted noise. Another huge plus of the dual-coil pickup is the chunky, fat sound beloved of rock and blues players. This design is still used by Gibson and remains unchanged to this day.

Other notable designs include the Gibson P-90, or **soap-bar** pickup, which sounds much like it looks—a fat single coil. It has a powerful tone but still retains much of the clarity of standard single-coils. **Active** pickups have also made quite an impact, with the EMG company being the largest manufacturer. These are available in humbucker and single-coil formats and use a battery powered **preamp** fitted inside the guitar. They produce a balanced clean sound with powerful

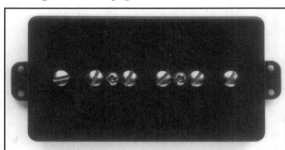

P-90 "soapbar" pickup

tone controls and excel at driving multiple effects for live and studio work.

There are a number of companies that specialize in making replacement pickups, the two largest being DiMarzio and Seymour Duncan. By modifying the wire and turns of the coil, the magnet and other parts of the pickup, they can offer a huge range of units with different tones. Some are designed to match vintage pickups very closely, which are ideal replacements in older instruments; others

have unique or modern tones. Charts describing the characteristics of each pickup can be obtained from their respective manufacturers.

Finally, it is worth mentioning the **piezo** pickup systems. Piezos

EMG active pickups

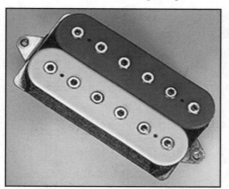

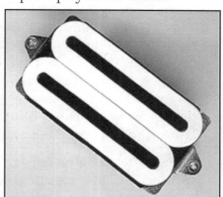

DiMarzio pickups

were once exclusively the domain of **electro-acoustic** guitars. These under-saddle pickups capture the acoustic properties of the instrument. Recently they have become increasingly common on solid-body electric guitars, such as the Parker Fly, where they can produce an authentic

Parker Fly guitar with piezo and electric pickups

43

acoustic sound. By blending this sound with that of the electric pickups, complex and exciting tones can be produced from one single instrument.

Electrics

The controls and switches fitted to a guitar all govern the pickups in some way. Some guitars have separate volume and tone controls for each pickup. Others share master controls or a combination, such as separate tone controls and a master volume. Pickup selector switches allow each of the pickups to be used individually or together. These may be individual on/off switches or, more commonly, one switch with three to five positions. For example the **five-way switch** on a Stratocaster operates the three pickups in the following sequence: bridge, bridge and center, center, center and neck, neck—producing five distinct sounds.

Other switches found on electric guitars are **coil taps**, **coil splitters** and **phase switches**. A coil tap selects a connection in the middle of a single-coil pickup winding, thereby using only half of the coil. This produces a quieter, cleaner sound with lots of high frequencies. A coil splitter is used on humbuckers to select just one of the two coils, producing a single-coil sound from a dual-coil pickup. Phase switches change the direction of the current in one coil with respect to another, the same direction being **in phase** and opposite directions being **out of phase**. In would be too complicated to cover all the permutations of phase switching, but essentially it can be used to reduce background noise or produce different tones that have a characteristically hollow "clucky" sound.

Different Types

6
5
4
3
2
1

By now you should be able to pick up a guitar and recognize all of the various parts and understand how they function. Through the descriptions of the different components you will hopefully have also realized how they all contribute to the all-important tone and feel of the guitar. The zillions of guitars available today offer endless permutations of these features, but certain recipes have stood the test of time better than others. If we look at some of the most popular classic designs more closely we can see how different the outcome is from putting certain parts together.

The **Gibson Les Paul** has a heavy mahogany body that imparts a warm, fat tone to the guitar. The body is capped with a maple top, and the addition of this wood helps to add brightness for a fuller, more balanced sound. The weight of the body, the fixed bridge and the glued-in neck all add a lot of sustain to the guitar, something the Les Paul is renowned for. The choice of pickups is two humbuckers, at the neck and bridge. These have a warm sound with a high output. The end result is a guitar with a powerful, full-bodied and solid tone that is both punchy and capable of long, sustained notes. This guitar works very well with overdrive and distortion sounds and is the choice of many rock players for its huge, heavy sound. The downside of this Gibson behemoth is that some players find the thick tone overbearing, as the powerful nature of the guitar makes it less dynamic than more restrained instruments.

The **Fender Stratocaster** could be considered the virtual opposite of the Les Paul in terms of sound and construc-

tion. When Leo Fender first designed the Stratocaster he kept ease of production and efficiency very much in mind. As a result the bodies of these guitars were made out of a number of readily available hardwoods such as alder, poplar and ash. The futuristic body design is a masterpiece of ergonomics: Leo simply took a slab of wood and removed all the parts that got in the way. The outcome was a sleek body with contours for the rib cage, forearm and hands of the player. Incidentally, the trademark headstock is a far-from-modern design—similar six-a-side pegheads appeared on acoustic guitars made in the mid-1800s.

As this was to be a production-line instrument, the one-piece neck was to be made separately and bolted on for the sake of efficiency. Similarly, the three single-coil pickups were integrated with the pickguard and the whole unit dropped into place. Although Leo wasn't chasing the ultimate tone from his mass-produced Strats, he certainly hit pay dirt, as most of the world's players agree he did just that.

The characteristic sound of the Strat comes from its light, resonant body and bolt-on neck, which adds punch. The combination of the trem and single-coil pickups gives it a loose and expressive sound with plenty of dynamics. The pickups are arranged with five selections, each having a particular flavor, from bright and snappy at the bridge to soft and woody at the neck. This comfortable and flexible instrument has found success in many different styles of music, although the pickups can sound thin and noisy with very high-gain sounds. This remains the best-selling electric guitar ever made.

Leo Fender also made a lot of players happy with the **Telecaster**. This simple guitar was the forerunner of the Stratocaster and shares many of its production techniques, albeit in less refined form. The Tele has a slab solid body with a single cutaway and a maple bolt-on neck. The original version had only one single-coil pickup integrated into the fixed bridge; this was later supplemented by a second one at the neck. The Tele is renowned for its twangy tone and sharp bite that has made it a firm favorite for country players. When used with an overdriven amp, the Telecaster produces a sinewy, acoustic-on-steroids rhythm sound that endeared it to rockers like Bruce Springsteen. Blues greats Albert Collins and Rory Gallagher loved its attack for lead work. It may not be the prettiest guitar, but this old workhorse is sure to be around for another 50 years.

Another type of guitar with a definite sound of its own is the semi. The **ES-335** is one of Gibson's most popular models and was introduced as a thinner-bodied version of their older jazz-style guitars. As such it is an evolved version of the electrified acoustic guitar, having a hollow body but sharing many features of a solid electric. Guitarist, recording inventor and innovative tinkerer Les Paul had a big impact on the guitar world and was even honored with his namesake Gibson. He had experimented with attaching pickups to a solid section of wood running the length of the guitar. This proved very successful and meant that body design was no longer dictated by acoustic considerations.

To demonstrate this he used a homemade guitar known as "The Log." It featured the pickups attached to a central block of pine. During a performance he would astonish the audience by discarding the removable acoustic sides of the guitar while it continued to function perfectly, even though it resembled nothing more than a lump of wood with an attached neck.

Many slim-bodied semis use this central block in their design to improve sustain while eliminating feedback, a common problem with fully acoustic bodies. However, the acoustic chambers on each side of the ES-335, complete with traditional F-shaped sound holes, add a characteristic resonance and jangle to the guitar's tone. The glued-in neck, humbuckers and fixed bridge add sustain and chunk, producing an instrument that is both dynamic and powerful. The ES-335's ability to play mellow one second and snarl the next has won it many friends in blues, rock, jazz and pop. This flexible instrument can be slightly hard to control at high volume and high gain, but this added chaos can inject some attitude into a performance.

The type of guitar described as a **Superstrat** has really evolved from its appearance in the '80s to include a vast number of instruments that blur the line between traditional Gibson and Fender designs. Eddie Van Halen is often credited for the concept of these hybrid guitars after he took a humbucker out of an ES-335 and squeezed it into the bridge position of a Strat-style body with the help of a chisel. With the addition of a modern, bolt-on neck and trem system, he produced an instrument that was perfect for the pyrotechnics of his style. The humbucker gave the guitar a much beefier tone than a Strat without being overly thick, but kept a tough, bright edge.

This design became a blueprint for companies such as Jackson and Kramer, who produced high-performance guitars using the humbucker, trem and bolt-on configuration. Since then most companies, including Fender and Gibson, have built guitars that mix up the traditional recipes and combine different pickups, bodies, and neck types with hi-tech hardware. These are no longer Superstrats, simply modern guitars that meld efficient design with vintage and cutting-edge sounds. With every conceivable combination having been covered by some manufacturer or another, there are plenty of these hybrid designs to choose from, each with its own range of sounds. If you are chasing a particular vintage feel and tone, then a traditional design is often the way to go. If you think of a Les Paul as having a red sound and a Strat as being green, then mixing the two together doesn't give you a color that is equally bright red and bright green, but more a mid-brown. In other words, a hybrid guitar is a compromise that will be able to approximate a number of guitars but will never sound, or behave, exactly the same as the originals. The upside is that these modern guitars can be easier to play and have a flat character. This allows you to develop your style without making allowances for the shortcomings of traditional designs, such as tuning stability, pickup noise and cumbersome necks. The flat tonal character is also a benefit as it lends itself to the use of complex effects as well as to the recording studio.

Oddballs and Newcomers

You will probably have surmised that guitar designers don't mind being radical from time to time. Aside from some of the unusual guitars already mentioned, there are still plenty of designs, old and new, that have the ability to make your jaw drop. Possibly the greatest rock star pose has to be the double-neck. Who could forget Jimmy Page and his Stairway to Heaven Gibson EDS-1275 6/12? Designed for live work, such instruments allow the

player to switch from one instrument to the other without changing guitar. They normally combine a 6-string neck with a 12-string on a single body, although some include bass or acoustic necks instead.

Twelve-string guitars double each string for a thick lush sound, but there are also variations on this design. Some guitars have only the top strings doubled, resulting in nine- or ten-string instruments, giving shimmery chords with more easily controlled bass strings. Other guitars, like the modern seven-string Ibanez Universe, just add an extra bass string for more low-end grind. Guitars with more than six strings are certainly more challenging to play, but their enriched sound, or added range, can be very inspiring.

12-string Rickenbacker

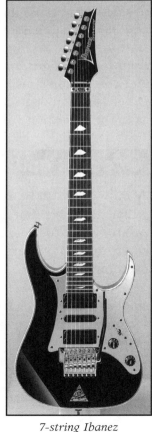

A particularly exciting development to check out is the guitar **synthesizer**. These appeared in the late '70s and required a dedicated guitar **controller**. Many players became disillusioned with their unreliability.

7-string Ibanez

But with recent developments in software and engineering it is now possible to hook up to a very powerful system with the  addition of just a simple pickup. These pickups are **hexaphonic** —usually a small clip-on unit containing a tiny pickup for each string—and they are used to control digital guitar synthesizers like those made by Roland. These systems digitally model the revered tones of classic guitars and amps, as well as other instruments, all from your own guitar. These systems may not be cheap, but they can make your humble Strat sound like a classical guitar, a 12-string acoustic, a Les Paul through a wall of Marshalls, a small orchestra, or even a one-man bongo beach party. Mind-blowing stuff indeed.

It is not possible to describe the sound and performance of every guitar you may come across as there are so many guitars and so many variables. The nature of guitar construction, and the materials used, can mean that even consecutively made, identical production-line instruments can sound surprisingly different. All of the above information will certainly give you a clearer idea of what to expect from a particular model, but the acid test is your own ears and fingers.

Buyer's Guide

By now you should understand why your particular guitar sounds and operates the way it does, and have an idea what instruments should be on your check-out list. Here are two more things that are quite important to keep in mind:

1. *Playing the same guitars as your heroes won't make you sound like them.* Most of a player's sound comes from his or her individual style. Hendrix sounded like Hendrix even when he played a ukulele. Also, the sounds you hear on record could come from any number of instruments, amps and production techniques the artist used for recording. By all means use your favorite player's model as a starting point, but make sure it works for you too.

2. *There are no rules when it comes to guitars.* Some models are associated with certain styles—fat-bodied semis for jazz, Flying Vs for heavy metal—but an open-minded approach can pay off. Many players found their trademark style through using "inappropriate" guitars, such as Ted Nugent's howling feedback from the previously jazz-only Gibson Byrdland and Lonnie Mack's legendary blues tone from his loyal Flying V, not to mention the grunge-approved Fender Jaguar, originally the obvious choice for sugary surf pop.

The bottom line is that whatever guitar you have, or want, has the ability to unlock your own style, as long as you enjoy playing it. With that out of the way, let's look at some pointers to help you find the type of instrument most likely to suit your applications.

If you are just starting out on the guitar, then the music store can be a confusing and intimidating place. Before you rush in with a fat wallet and an eager grin, it is best to do some research first. Every guitar store has something unpleasant hanging up in the stock room, and an unprepared customer with a fistful of cash can miraculously change this unsellable dog into the perfect guitar—according to the salesperson. With a bit of thought and bookwork you can be confident about your purchase and enjoy guitar shopping—one of life's greatest pleasures!

What You Need

To begin your guitar-buying adventure you need to establish what features you need on the instrument. We've covered the main differences in the sound and structure of the models you will come across, so you should have an idea of which guitars could suit you best. To recap, your main considerations should be:

Tremolo or Fixed Bridge

If you want the trem to be part of your technique, then you'll obviously need one on your guitar. Remember that vintage versions will work best for more subtle techniques with a vintage tone. If you lean toward more modern, aggressive styles, then you should consider looking into guitars with high-performance systems that include locking, roller or graphite parts in the design.

Single Coils or Humbuckers

If you want to play with a lot of distortion, then humbuckers are usually the first choice. For lower-gain and clean sounds, the more open tone of single coils can add a bit more texture to your playing. If you intend to play a number of styles, guitars with a combination of both should be on your list.

Vintage or Modern

If you are looking for pure classic tones you should look to the vintage designs outlined in Chapter 4. Players aiming to shred should check out guitars like those made by Ibanez and Jackson, which are designed for rock and metal styles.

You may also find that modern designs offer you greater flexibility in terms of different tones.

Other aspects of the design are down to personal taste and preferences. Take your time to read brochures and guitar magazine reviews, talk to other players and window-shop to collect as much info as you can before buying. This way you can target models with the features you want and compare prices.

Budget

Once you have an idea of the style of guitar you want, you then need to establish your budget—the highest figure you can afford to spend. Guitar production has improved so much over the last decade that many companies now offer excellent, well-made guitars for those on a tight budget. At one time budget guitars made in the Far East were frowned upon, but these days these overseas plants make some very respectable instruments while saving you bucks.

It is safe to assume

that guitars in the entry-level to mid-priced range (around $200 to $600) have price tags that reflect their quality and hardware. As you pay more you can expect to get a guitar with better parts, better woods and more attention to detail. However, you can still expect a solid wood body, functional hardware, good playability and a reasonable tone from an entry-level guitar.

Guitars in the mid-to-upper price range (around $600 to $1,200) should be outfitted with high-quality hardware and woods, and models in this range are normally offered with more options than cheaper guitars. Although you may not get the most ostentatious of ornamentation, you can still expect interesting finishes and woods. This is the most competitive area of the market, so there are many models to choose from in a large range of styles. Some of the best values in professional-quality guitars are found in this price range.

Instruments falling into the highest price range (around $1,200 to $10,000 or more) are usually those made by the top companies in the U.S. and Japan. These will have top-name hardware and use premium woods, often figured, in addition to more labor-intensive production methods. In this case a considerable amount of your money will go toward the look of the instrument—e.g., carved tops, flamed maple, intricate inlays and time-consuming finishes. Many compa-

nies will offer such models as **custom shop pieces**, meaning they are largely hand-built and you can specify many, if not all, of the options. As wonderful as some of these instruments are, common sense should tell you that a $10,000 custom shop model is not actually 10 times better than the basic $1,000 production model.

Once you have established how much you want to spend, keep an open mind and consider guitars priced below your budget as well. You may find what you need for a lot less. If you are buying your first guitar, it wouldn't be sensible to blow your life savings on a custom shop masterpiece. Like most purchases, guitars depreciate in value as soon as they are bought. Very few players stick with their first guitar, finding that as their technique and style develop, so do their tastes. Concentrate on finding an instrument that you find easy to play, with an enjoyable tone, and at a reasonable price.

Essential Checklist

No matter what guitar you decide to buy, and whatever your budget, the following points should be checked and passed. If any of these items are not satisfactory, the guitar could be a lemon—in other words, a very bad investment.

☐ Neck

This needs to be straight and free of humps or twists. Check that a neck is not warped by sighting along its length using the strings as a guide. Do this by looking down the neck from the nut to the bridge at a nearly flat angle. If the neck appears to twist away from the strings, or is noticeably higher in places, then you will have problems.

☐ Frets

Inspect the frets to ensure that none have slipped out of their slots, and that none of them are loose. The ends should be free of any sharp edges and all the frets should be smooth and polished. You can check for warping and bad frets by fretting every string at every fret, preferably while bending the string. Any dull or buzzy frets mean extra work is needed before the guitar will play properly.

☐ Setup

Any new guitar should have been set up properly prior to sale. Check that the action is comfortably low and free of buzzes and rattles. The above every string/every fret test will also uncover a bad setup, so check that notes ring properly across the whole neck. If the guitar has a tremolo, test it for creaks and clicks, which could mean it's sticking. Also check that the trem has a positive movement and returns to its resting position easily and with a minimum of detuning.

☐ Electrics

Plug the guitar in and try all of the switches and controls. These should work without crackling or cutting out. Try playing through all of the pickup selections and be wary of unacceptable levels of background hum. If there is a lot of buzzing coming from the amp, then the guitar may not be properly grounded and could be fatal—don't take chances!

☐ Construction

Take a good look at the instrument, checking for cracks or splits in the wood. Look carefully at the neck-to-body joint; cracks appearing here could mean the instrument was dropped during shipping.

If the guitar has a bolt-on neck, make sure the pocket is tight-fitting. Tiny gaps in this area could lead to problems, so check to be sure there is no sideways movement in the neck. Most obviously, a new guitar should be free of scratches or chips in the finish.

☐ Hardware

In addition to checking the movement of the trem, make sure any other moving parts (fine tuners, rollers, trem arm, etc.) all operate freely. Have a close look at fixed bridges too. Both types need to be checked for damaged or loose parts. Machine heads should feel firm and smooth when turned.

If your guitar passes the above checklist then you have little to worry about. Use your common sense when checking out a guitar; sloppy work on the outside probably means that hidden work, like wiring and routing, is even worse. If the guitar is fit and healthy, feels good to play, makes some fine noise and the color suits you, it's time to haggle. Go for a good deal. Most stores will drop the price or throw in a case, so it's worth trying your luck. Don't forget the receipt and a warranty, just in case.

Used Guitars

This topic warrants a guide of its own, not least because it covers a multitude of guitars, from a $50 yard sale junker to Jimi Hendrix's 1968 "Woodstock" Stratocaster, which was sold for nearly $340,000. To be realistic we'll look at the basic pros and cons of buying secondhand guitars, as opposed to the cutthroat world of vintage collecting.

For players on a budget, buying used can save you a considerable amount. Once a guitar has been sold its value will drop to a fairly standard secondhand price, which means that, if you look after it, you should be able to resell it without a loss. Another benefit of used guitars is their "played-in" feel, an unquantifiable quality that gives guitars with a few miles on the clock a certain amount of character and smoother playability. This character also tends to include a few dents, scratches and other battle scars.

The real downside of buying used is some people's tendency to do utterly horrible things to their instruments. You may be able to live with a psychotic paint job or lame stickers, but amateur custom work can render electronics unusable and the structure unsound. Be wary of any guitar that has been tampered with. Its value will certainly have been reduced and it may be unsafe. If you buy from a store, ask if it has had a safety checkup and comes with a warranty. If you buy privately, then budget for a checkup by your local guitar repairer. Pay extra attention for any signs of wear, damage or repair—a bargain can quickly become a money drain if you have to spend $200 for a refret and another $100 for rewiring. If a guitar looks beat up, then it hasn't been looked after and it could be a minefield of problems. If you have your doubts, look elsewhere.

Mail Order

Finally, a quick word about buying over the phone or the Internet. Many people don't have a local store, or the time for a day trip to visit one. In this case, mail order can be the only option. The main problem with this method is not being able to try the guitar you want to buy. It may seem perfect from the catalogue blurb, but you could well hate it minutes after it turns up on your doorstep. Thankfully, many stores offer a return policy that allows you to exchange the guitar for a refund or another model. Be sure to check if the store offers this, and what conditions apply. Shopping privately for used equipment can be risky. If you are buying or selling in response to a private ad, always establish the terms first and have everything sent by registered courier to avoid "lost" guitars or checks. Use common sense and be careful.

Maintenance **6.**

By now your guitar should no longer be a baffling contraption but a friendly instrument whose habits and inner workings you understand. This should help you spot any problems as they occur, but with some simple maintenance there is no reason why your guitar shouldn't last a lifetime.

Cleaning and Storage

One of the best investments for protecting your guitar is a soft cleaning cloth, available very cheap from any music store. Get into the habit of wiping the whole guitar down after every playing session. Sweat is slightly acidic and is most unkind to strings, frets, fretboards and hardware. By wiping over your guitar, not forgetting to slide the cloth under the strings to reach everything, you will remove most of the sweat and dust that can cause problems. This will prolong the life of your strings and prevent dirt from building up on the fretboard and between moving parts. Periodically treat your guitar to a polish using one of the guitar finish polishes available. Don't be tempted to use domestic cleaning products. Fingerboards can be cleaned, nourished and protected by a regular wipe-down with lemon oil or similar guitar products sold in music stores.

The best place to store your guitar is in its case, or if you don't have one, the original cardboard box. Leaving you guitar precariously balanced against a chair is inviting headstock-snapping horror scenes as well as a thick layer of dust. A hard

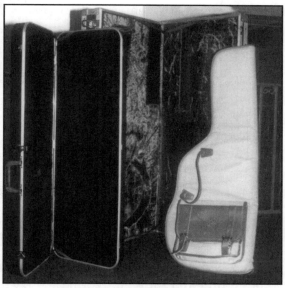

Soft, hard and flight cases

case is the best insurance for guitars, especially if you intend to take them out of the house. As wood is sensitive to changes in temperature and humidity, there are some other rules when it comes to storage: Never leave your guitar near a radiator or other heater. Never leave it in damp places, such as cold basements or garages, and, except during outdoor performances, keep it out of direct sunlight.

Tuning

Tuning your guitar is absolutely essential to playing, and any elementary book will show you a number of methods to do this. It can be very frustrating, especially with trem-equipped guitars, but it becomes second nature with practice. You can use a **pitch pipe**, **tuning fork** or piano to match your A string to the correct or "concert" pitch, then tune the other strings to that note. Having someone show you how to do this really helps. If, like most beginners, you find this difficult, one solution is to buy an **electronic tuner**. These can be bought for as little as $30 and make tuning fast, accurate and easy. They also help you to recognize the correct pitch of tuned strings, but do take the time to learn how to tune by ear so you don't have to rely on a tuner all the time.

Changing Strings

After a while you will notice that your guitar is starting to sound dull and the strings appear dirty and tarnished.

This means it's time for a string change. In addition to replacing broken strings, it is essential to put a new set of strings on your guitar regularly, as tired old strings can make the guitar sound out of tune and muddy. There are lot of different strings to choose from: stainless steel, nickel, hexagonal core, and even gold-plated. You will find the brand you prefer simply through experience, but the most important consideration is the **gauge**.

String gauge is traditionally measured in 1,000ths of an inch, with the thinnest—high E—string as a reference. In this way a **nine set** refers to a set of strings starting with 0.009"-thick E string and a "ten set" would be have a 0.010" E, with the other five strings being correspondingly heavier as well. These are more helpfully called **extra-light** and **light** gauges, respectively. There are also medium, heavy and extra-heavy gauges with sets starting as high as 0.014". These tiny differences in string gauge may not sound like much, but they feel very different. The heavier the gauge, the stiffer the feel, so beginners should start with the lightest sets as they are easier to play and often remain the choice of many players. So why use heavy strings? Because they improve tone by being louder and more responsive, with increased sustain. If you intend to

String winders

try heavy strings, work up through the gauges gradually or you could strain and damage your hands.

Changing strings may be a pain, but the improved tone is worth it and with time you will be able to do it very quickly. The only tool you need for the job is a pair of wire cutters, although I recommend spending a few dollars on a **string winder**, which makes restringing faster and smoother. If you don't need to clean your fretboard then it is best to change one string at a time. Starting with the thickest—low E—string, slacken it off with the machine head, then cut it near the bridge and remove. Feed the new string through the bridge (or clamp the snipped end down for Floyd Rose systems), then pass

69

the other end through the hole in the machine head post. Leave enough slack to wind the string onto the post—as a guide, pull the string taut away from the neck and pull through the post hole until there is a 10-cm gap between the string and the 12th fret. Keeping tension on the string, slowly wind up the slack counterclockwise on six-a-side headstocks (counterclockwise for the three bass strings and clockwise for the top three strings on three-a-side headstocks). Make sure the windings are neat and move downward without overlapping. Once the string becomes taut, snip off the excess to about 10 mm from the post. The thicker bottom strings should have three or four turns around the post; the higher strings should have between five and seven turns. Any more than this can cause tuning problems; any less and the strings can begin to slip off the post. Once the strings are fitted, lightly stretch and retune them a few times until they settle in tune.

Repairs to Expect

If you look after your guitar as described above and avoid dropping it, then you should keep trips to the workshop to a minimum. However, as the guitar has moving parts, including the strings, a certain amount of wear is inevitable, which requires repair work.

Over time the frets get worn into pits beneath the strings, causing buzzing and a lumpy feel. This is remedied by having the frets lightly ground and polished by a repairer. This wear takes quite a while to develop and the frets can normally withstand three or four of these **dressings** before a more expensive **refret** is required.

It is also wise to have your guitar checked and setup every year or two. As it is played, parts move, electrical contacts get dirty and other general wear and tear occurs. By having a repairer service your guitar, he can replace any worn parts, clean electrical components and adjust the setup to ensure the guitar plays and sounds its best.

Upgrading Hardware and Modifications

After playing your guitar for some time you may find that you want to improve or change some features. It may be that it has cheaper unsealed machine heads that drift out of tune, which you want to upgrade to sealed versions. You may decide to change the pickups for some with a better tone. Or you might just want a funky-looking pickguard for the sake of individuality. In most cases these modifications can be done easily using a variety of parts designed to retro-fit your guitar, as long as you are confident with your hands, and, in the case of electrical parts, can wield a soldering iron with a rudimentary knowledge of electronics. If you are in any doubt about performing a modification, then leave it to a repairman. It may cost a little more but you won't risk messing up your guitar.

When you are considering making modifications, be sure to weigh the cost. If you intend to upgrade the pickups, machine heads and pickguard, for example, you will proba-bly find it is cheaper to sell or trade your guitar in for another with the features you want. If you decide to change any parts, try to keep the original parts safe so you can return the guitar to its original form—very important for collectible instruments. Be especially wary of modifications that permanently alter the structure of the guitar, such as those requiring extra routing. Seek advice first to be aware of the implications of such modifications. Even Eddie Van Halen managed to ruin the tone of one of his favorite guitars with an ill-informed mod.

Tinkering and customizing is a fun sideline for many players, but remember that faulty wiring and power tools are dangerous, and guitars are expensive things. If you intend to embark on any major projects, get some advice and read one of the repair guides available before you start. If it sounds like more than you can handle, leave it to a repairer, because it will probably end up there anyway.

Learning to Play 7

Now that you know how the thing works, you're probably itching to know how you can make it work. There are a multitude of teaching aids available to help you on the road to guitar mastery, and any one of them will help your playing improve. If you're an absolute beginner, a few one-on-one lessons can really help you over the hurdles of grasping the rudimentary techniques. You may wish to continue with regular lessons or attend one of the many courses available. Otherwise there is lots of material to help you teach yourself and concentrate on the styles you wish to learn.

Instructional Aids

There are a number of comprehensive beginner's guides in book, video and computer software formats. Videos have the advantage of being able to demonstrate hand positions and fingering with movement and close-ups. Computer software, especially **CD-ROMs**, is an expanding field for guitar tuition. Many of these multimedia packages include Real-Time video close-ups in combination with a graphic representation of the fretboard and musical notation. Some CD-ROM systems even allow you to hook your guitar up to the computer to interact and monitor progress.

Guitarists are somewhat spoiled when it comes to music, as we also have a simplified notation of our very own. Known as **TAB**, this system depicts the music as numbers on six horizontal lines. The numbers correspond to frets and the lines represent the six strings starting with high E at the top. There is a wealth of guitar music available in this format, normally accompanied by standard notation, and it can be found in books or guitar magazines and downloaded from the Internet. Once you have a basic understanding of guitar playing, this system makes it very easy to cop your favorite players' licks.

Practice and Progressing

Although it may seem obvious, practice really is the key to developing your skills on the guitar. Whichever instructional method you use, be sure to work through it methodically and practice all the exercises to get the most from the system. The simple truth is, the more you play, the better you will become. Whether you do some serious woodshedding with a metronome or just noodle in front of the TV, it all helps you to improve.

Try to develop a practice regimen of your own. This should include warm-up exercises to prevent strains, and dividing time equally between various techniques: chords, scales, rhythm, left-hand fingering, right-hand picking, etc. If you find any technique particularly difficult, then pinpoint and gradually work on it until there is no longer a problem.

One of the best and most enjoyable ways of developing your skills is to play with other musicians. Try to find other players to **jam** with. It doesn't matter what level they are at—everyone will benefit. This way you can put what you've learned into practice and try out techniques in an actual musical setting. This helps you to think on your feet as you accompany (comp) and improvise (solo), and painlessly helps you develop your timing and phrasing. It's also a lot more fun than a metronome—and that, at the end of the day, should be what playing guitar is all about: fun.

Additional Guides from Hal Leonard Corporation

The Complete History of Epiphone
by Walter Carter
00330033 ....(146 pages, 9" X 12") $22.95

The Fender Book: A Complete History of Fender Electric Guitars
2nd Edition
by Tony Bacon & Paul Day
00330459 ....(120 pages, 7" X 9-3/4") $24.95

The Fender Stratocaster
by A. R. Duchossoir, foreword by Eric Clapton
00330027 ....(72 pages, 9" X 12") $14.95

The Fender Telecaster
by A. R. Duchossoir, special foreword by James Burton and Albert Lee
00183003 ....(80 pages, 9" X 12") $14.95

Gibson Electrics: The Classic Years–Revised
An Illustrated History of the Electric Guitars Produced by Gibson up to the Mid-1960s
by A. R. Duchossoir
00330392 ....(256 pages, 9" X 12") $24.95

The Gibson Les Paul Book
by Tony Bacon & Paul Day
00330101 ....(96 pages, 7" X 9-3/4") $22.95

The Gibson Super 400
by Thomas A. Van Hoose
00330124 ....(195 pages, 8" X 11") $24.95

Gretsch
The Guitars of the Fred Gretsch Co.
by Jay Scott
00000142...(286 pages, 9"X12") $35.00

The Gretsch Book
A Complete History of Gretsch Electric Guitars
by Tony Bacon & Paul Day
00330226 ....(108 pages, 7" X 9-3/4") $24.95

The Guild Guitar Book
The Company and the Instruments–1952-1977
by Han Moust
00330502 ....(184 pages, 9-1/4" X 12") $39.95

The Martin Book
by Walter Carter
00330149 ....(108 pages, 7-1/2" X 9-3/4") $22.95

The History of Ovation
by Walter Carter
00330187 ....(128 pages, 9" X 12") $22.95

Rickenbacker
by Richard Smith
00000098 ....(256 pages, 9" X 12") $29.95

The Rickenbacker Book–A Complete History of Rickenbacker Electric Guitars
by Tony Bacon & Paul Day
00330200 ....(96 pages, 7-1/2" X 9-3/4") $19.95

Acoustic Guitars and Other Fretted Instruments –A Photographic History
by George Gruhn & Walter Carter
00330343 ....(320 pages, 8-3/4" X 11-1/2") $29.95

Classic Guitars of the '50s
00330253 ....(88 pages 10-1/4" X 12-7/8") $29.95

Classic Guitars of the '60s
How the Electric Guitar and Its Players Dominated a Revolutionary Decade of Mind-Blowing Music
00330393 ....(88 pages 10-1/4" X 12-7/8") $29.95

The Guitar Handbook
The Essential Encyclopedia for Every Guitar Player
by Ralph Denyer
00330105 ....(256 pages, 8-1/2" X 11") $25.00

Guitar Identification–Revised 3rd Edition
by Andre Duchossoir
00330478 ....(64 pages, 9" X 12") $9.95

Guitars That Shook the World
by the editors of Guitar World magazine
00330119 ....(128 pages, 9" X 12") $19.95

For More Information, See Your Local Music Dealer,
Or Write To:

HAL•LEONARD®
CORPORATION
7777 W. Bluemound Rd. P.O. Box 13819 Milwaukee, WI 53213

Visit our website at
www.halleonard.com

Guitar World Presents: The Bonehead's Guides

The Bonehead's Guide to Guitars

by Dominic Hilton

Don't know your tremolo from your truss rod? Fear not, this book will guide you through the essential differences between various electric guitars with clear explanations of how they work, how they sound and how their parts function. Learn about the effect that different construction, woods and components have on the tone of a guitar, and how to use this knowledge to get the most from your instrument or track down your ideal electric.

This guide also includes vital information on which guitar to choose for your style of playing and budget, and how to avoid buying a problem instrument. It also contains valuable advice on maintaining and upgrading your guitar, and covers all of the safety precautions associated with using an electrified instrument.
00695332 .... $9.95

The Bonehead's Guide to Amps

by Dominic Hilton

For many novice players their amp is the boring, functional part of their first setup. This guide explains how it can be as exciting, inspirational and important as their guitar. Viewing the amp as an instrument in its own right, this book defines both the fundamental and subtle differences between many types of amplifiers, while offering valuable info on "tone-tweaking" every kind to suit different styles. Learn how to adjust your amp for a whole range of different tones and how to use its functions to maximum effect.

By taking an objective and comprehensive view of available guitar amps, this book offers the best bang-for-buck advice on getting killer tones easily, affordably and blasting at the right level. If you want to get your guitar cooking, then make sure it has the right ingredients with this invaluable guide.
00695334 .... $9.95

The Bonehead's Guide to Effects

by Dominic Hilton

The bizarre technology of guitar effects uses everything from feet to floppy disks, and this guide provides the necessary knowledge to choose and apply these weird devices according to your style and budget. If you feel the urge to wah, flange, uni-vibe or pitch-shift, then this is the book to get you effected.

The Bonehead's Guide to Effects gets right to the point with an illustrated description of every type of guitar effect, including its sound, application and the various formats available. From a simple "stompbox" to high-powered rack systems, all are clearly explained in terms of how they function and how they can be used to enhance your playing.

The text includes a detailed buyer's guide to assembling your ideal effects system, alongside useful safety and maintenance tips. There is also vital info on "chaining" effects and recipes for basic tones and outrageous sounds.
00695333 .... $9.95

GUITAR WORLD

PRESENTS

Guitar World Presents is an ongoing series of books filled with extraordinary interviews, feature pieces and instructional material that have made *Guitar World* magazine the world's most popular musicians' magazine. For years, *Guitar World* has brought you the most timely, the most accurate and the most hard-hitting news and views about your favorite players. Now you can have it all in one convenient package: *Guitar World Presents*.

Guitar World Presents Classic Rock
00330370 (304 pages, 6" x 9") $17.95

Guitar World Presents Alternative Rock
00330369 (352 pages, 6" x 9") $17.95

Guitar World Presents Nirvana and the Grunge Revolution
00330368 (240 pages, 6" x 9") $16.95

Guitar World Presents Kiss
00330291 (144 pages, 6" x 9") $14.95

Guitar World Presents Van Halen
00330294 (208 pages, 6" x 9") $14.95

Guitar World Presents Metallica
00330292 (144 pages, 6" x 9") $14.95

Guitar World Presents Stevie Ray Vaughan
00330293 (144 pages, 6" x 9") $14.95